PICTURE LIBRARY

KARTING

PICTURE LIBRARY
KARTING

Norman Barrett

Franklin Watts

London   New York   Sydney   Toronto

© 1988 Franklin Watts Ltd

First published in Great Britain
    1988 by
Franklin Watts Ltd
12a Golden Square
London W1R 4BA

First published in the USA by
Franklin Watts Inc
387 Park Avenue South
New York
NY 10016

First published in Australia by
Franklin Watts
14 Mars Road
Lane Cove
NSW 2066

UK ISBN: 0 86313 681 8
US ISBN: 0-531-10630-6
Library of Congress Catalog Card
Number 88-50360

Printed in Italy

Designed by
Barrett & Willard

Photographs by
Doug Rees
Ed McCormick
Beverley Heath
Ashley Holding
Jonsport Photos
Ian Blair
Action Plus
Colin Stephens
N.S. Barrett Collection
World Karting Association

Illustrations by
Rhoda & Robert Burns

Technical Consultant
Ed McCormick

Contents

Introduction

Karting is an exciting motor sport for all ages. Boys and girls can take part from the age of about eight, and adults also enjoy the sport.

The kart is one of the simplest of motorized racing machines. It has a low chassis, and the driver sits not more than about an inch above the ground. Karts are powered by small engines, but the most powerful classes can reach speeds of 240 km/h (150 mph).

△ A powerful 250 cc kart looks almost like a racing car. At over 200 km/h (125 mph), it is certainly faster than any other kart on the road.

Karting is popular in Europe and North America. Long-circuit racing usually takes place on proper motor racing tracks, with circuits from 2.4 to 6.4 km (1½ to 4 miles) in length. There are many more short-circuit tracks, especially built for the sport.

In long-circuit racing, where there is plenty of room for overtaking, as many as 60 karts might start a race. In short-circuit racing, there is a limit of between 18 and 24.

△ A championship race for mixed classes. Several karts vie for position on the first bend. The wide tracks used in long-circuit racing allow as many as 60 starters.

The kart

The simplest kart has a 100 cc engine and no gearbox. The driver sits very close to the ground.

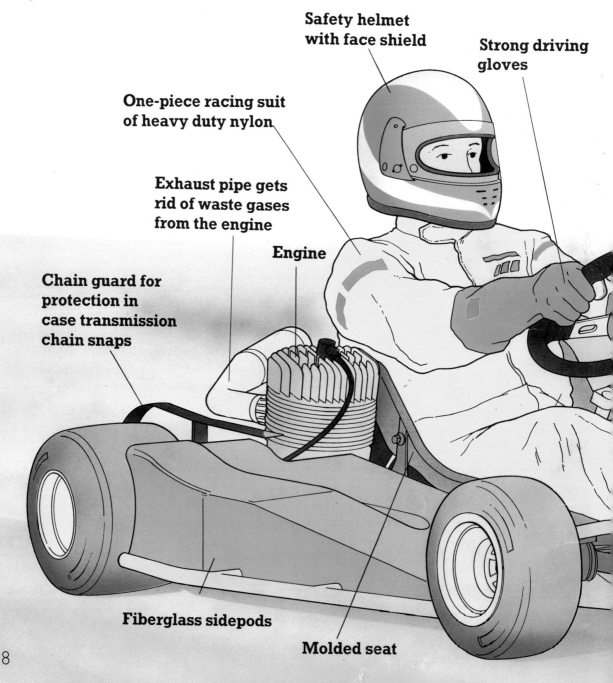

Safety helmet with face shield

Strong driving gloves

One-piece racing suit of heavy duty nylon

Exhaust pipe gets rid of waste gases from the engine

Engine

Chain guard for protection in case transmission chain snaps

Fiberglass sidepods

Molded seat

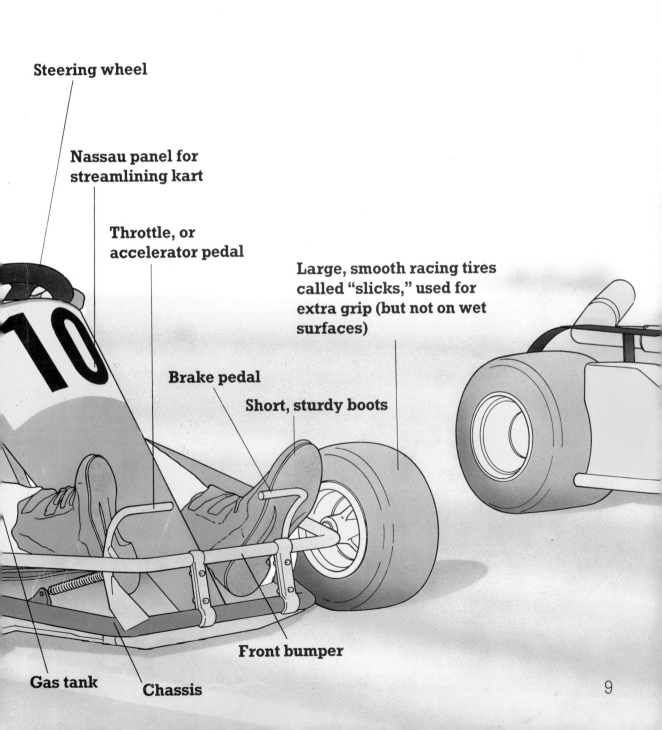

Steering wheel

Nassau panel for
streamlining kart

Throttle, or
accelerator pedal

Large, smooth racing tires
called "slicks," used for
extra grip (but not on wet
surfaces)

Brake pedal

Short, sturdy boots

Gas tank

Chassis

Front bumper

Starting karting

There are tracks where karts are available for rent to the public. Anyone can enjoy leisure karting, provided safety precautions are taken, such as the wearing of helmets.

For children and adults who want to take the sport more seriously, there are karting clubs which organize races and meetings. Clubs provide advice for beginners on racing and equipment.

▽ Some tracks offer leisure karting, where perhaps not every safety precaution is taken. A spill without a proper racing suit could lead to painful skin grazes.

Even a Junior Rookie class kart, for drivers aged 8–12, costs from $700 to $1,000. So karting is not a cheap hobby. But compared with other motor sports, it is a relatively inexpensive introduction to racing.

Other equipment includes a helmet, one-piece leather or heavy-duty racing nylon suit, racing boots and gloves. These are also not cheap, but are essential for good and safe driving.

△ A Junior Rookie kart race for 8 to 12 year-olds. In most countries where karting is popular, there are classes for youngsters. The karts are pretty fast and the racing is just as close and exciting as in the more powerful classes.

◁ In the lowest age groups, the karts are powered by 60 cc engines, and can reach speeds of over 70 km/h (45 mph) on the straight. They have a recoil starter, as in some lawnmowers, and there is no gear changing. Long-life tires are used to keep the cost of racing down.

This class of racing has an excellent safety record. With four wheels and a low center of gravity, karts are much more stable than trials and BMX.

How a race is run

Officials called tech inspectors ensure that all karts entered for a race are of safe construction, with brakes in working order. They also check that the drivers are wearing approved protective clothing.

Other course officials check the safety barriers and make sure that the track is free of hazardous materials. Officials called flagmen are posted on the bends to signal any danger.

▽ Off the track, there is a pit area where mechanics can work on the karts.

Races are started from a grid.
A kart's position on the starting grid
is determined by qualifying heats.
These heats are usually 4 to 6 laps,
with a final over 8 to 10 laps.

The karts line up off the track on a
dummy grid. They do a warm-up lap
at medium speed, keeping their grid
positions. Starts are controlled by
lights or flag signals. As soon as the
karts reach the grid in correct order,
the starter switches the lights from
red to green (or waves a flag).

△ Starting numbers are
marked on the dummy
grid. Drivers and
mechanics make last-
minute adjustments or
chat about tactics. In
European long-circuit
karting there are 3–5
karts on each row of the
grid.

15

△ A pace car takes the karts round on the warm-up lap before the start of a big long-circuit race at Silverstone, England, one of Europe's leading motor-racing tracks.

◁ On the narrow tracks of short-circuit racing, the karts line up on the grid in twos.

Racing

In Europe, direct drive karts – that is, karts without gearboxes – range from the 60 cc Cadet class to the international Formula K, which has a 135 cc engine.

Classes of karts with gearboxes range from 125 cc to 250 cc. The chief international class is Formula E, with its 250 cc engine. In the gearbox classes, most karts use standard motorcycle or motocross engines.

▽ The leading driver in a 100 cc race manages to keep control despite clipping the curb as he takes a hairpin bend. There are many sharp twists and turns in short-circuit racing, where the minimum width of the track is only 6 m (20 ft).

Asphalt tracks are used for both short- and long-circuit racing in Europe. The short-circuit tracks vary from about 400 m to 530 m (¼ to ⅓ miles).

In the United States long-circuit races are called enduros. Sprints are run on short asphalt circuits, speedway on dirt oval tracks. In speedway, a 400 m (¼ mile) circuit is a long track, a 160 m (¹⁄₁₀ mile) circuit a short track.

▽ Enduro racing at Daytona International Racetrack, Florida, with 100 cc karts.

△ Speedway, popular in the United States, is run on oval dirt tracks. On ⅛-mile tracks, there is plenty of bumping as drivers go for the inside. On ⅕-mile tracks, speeds of 120 km/h (75 mph) may be reached.

▷ Such are the speeds of these long-circuit 250 cc karts that they need aerofoils at the back to keep the wheels on the ground. They have streamlined bodies to cut down wind resistance.

▷ As these three open-wheel 135 cc karts come hurtling around a sharp turn, it looks as if they are touching. This is just a trick of the camera, but in short-circuit racing there is a certain amount of physical contact as several karts go for the inside lane at the same time on the narrow track.

◁ Out on her own, 10-year-old Clair Bogan wins the British Cadet Championship. In karting, girls compete with boys, women with men.

▽ In Europe there are karting events for teams. Points are given for finishing position, 1 for 1st, 2 for 2nd and so on, and the team with the fewest total points is the winner.

△ Sprint races in the United States are held mainly on twisting asphalt tracks with a great variety of left and right hand bends.

◁ If the engine cuts out for any reason, there's usually no alternative but to push the kart off the track to safety.

Championships

World championships for Formula E 250 cc karts are staged every year. There are three rounds, or grands prix, which are held on motor-racing tracks in different countries.

Point are awarded for each race – 15 for the winner, 12 for 2nd place, 10 for 3rd, 9 for 4th, 8 for 5th, down to 1 for 12th. The driver who gains most points in the three grands prix is the world champion.

△ Karts line up on the grid for a world championship grand prix. Drivers are allotted a grid position based on their practice times, and then compete in a "pre-finale" of at least 22 km (13.7 miles) or 6 laps to earn their position on the grid for the race. This is held over at least 45 km (28 miles) or 10 laps, whichever is the greater.

◁ The rewards in karting might not be the same as in grand prix motor racing, but the winners enjoy their celebrations just as much! Trophies, floral wreaths and champagne are the order of the day.

▽ Junior world championships are sometimes held as single races. This is a 100 cc event, at the famous Le Mans motor-racing circuit in France.

▷ A world
championship grand
prix at Hockenheim in
West Germany. Like
their big brothers in
motor racing, karts are
heavily sponsored in
major races. They lap
the track like fast-
moving advertising
boards. Karting might
be cheap to start with,
but running a grand prix
racing team runs into
several thousands of
dollars.

The story of karting

From go-cart to kart

The term go-cart has been used over the centuries for different kinds of vehicles. It was first used more than 300 years ago for a framework on casters with which a child could learn to walk without falling. Later, it came to mean a light open carriage.

Go-carts of a certain type have been used for years in the famous All-American Soap-Box Derby, held every year in Akron, Ohio, since before World War II. But this is a downhill coasting race for small motor-less racing cars.

When karting first became popular, the vehicles were called go-karts (spelled with a "k"). Now they are just called karts.

△ Youngsters race past the finish in the All-American Soap Box Derby, a popular event long before the invention of karts.

The karting craze

The kart was invented in 1956 in California by a racing car mechanic named Art Ingels and his friend Lou Borelli when they found some surplus 100 cc lawnmower engines. They made a simple framework from steel tubing, fixed four wheels on the corners and mounted an engine behind the driver's seat.

Test runs of this strange new machine without any bodywork had people of all ages eager to buy replicas or even building their own. Every week more and more karts appeared and the owners began to race them. The karting craze had begun. In no time at all, a karting club was formed, and then the first kart track was built, at Azusa, California.

Spread of the sport

Regular race meets began to be organized at air bases around the United States. When US airmen arrived in Britain, they brought their karting enthusiasm with them and introduced the sport to the British. Circuits started springing up in Britain in 1959–60, mainly at unused airfields. The sport caught on and soon spread to the rest of Europe. By 1970, almost every country had its karts and karters, in both Western and Eastern Europe.

World championships

It was not long after the invention of the kart that the first self-styled world championships were held in the United States. The first world karting title was won by Jimmy Yamane (US) in 1959.

Karts and karting developed on different lines inside and outside the United States, and soon a world governing body was set up in Europe called the Commission Internationale de Karting (CIK), based in Paris. The CIK organized the first true world championships in 1964 for 100 cc karts, won by Guido Sala of Italy.

In 1981, the world championship formula was changed from 100 cc to 135 cc displacement motors. Then, in 1983, another class was introduced, the Formula E for

△ Martin Hines driving with the treasured red No. 1 on a white number plate, which he earned when he won the first Formula E World Karting Championship.

250 cc "super" karts with gearboxes. The first title was won by British driver Martin Hines.

Nursery for racing drivers

Almost from the start, karting has turned out to be a "nursery" for racing drivers. Many of the world's leading Formula One motor racers cut their teeth on karting circuits before progressing to greater things. They include the 1974 karting champion and runner-up, Ricardo Patrese (Italy) and Eddie Cheever (US), and Ayrton Senna (Brazil), runner-up in 1979 and 1980.

Facts and records

Most world titles

Italian drivers have by far the best record in the non-gearbox Karting World Championships, including the first woman to win the title, Susanna Raganelli, in 1966. But the driver with the most world titles is a Belgian, François Goldstein, who won five times between 1969 and 1975.

"Drag" karting

Although there is no such thing as "drag karting," a head-to-head sprint between two karts over a short straight, some karts are built for record purposes. In 1987, a British student, Stuart Bond of Bath University, set two world records at Elvington, in North Yorkshire. In a 250 cc kart built by fellow students of Team Quanta, he completed ¼ mile (402 m) from a standing start in 12.775 sec. The next day he covered 1 km (0.62 mile) of the track in 27.088 seconds.

Endurance

An endurance record was set by a four-man Canadian team in 1983. They took turns driving a 140 cc kart 1,638.3 km (1,018 miles), around a twisting 1 mile (1.64 km) circuit at Erbsville Kartway, Ontario.

△ Stuart Bond at the start of the record ¼-mile run . . .

△ . . . at full speed . . .

△ . . . and in the same kart, but with the bodywork added, ready for the 1-km record.

Glossary

Aerofoil
A wing at the back of a kart designed so that the air rushing past pushes it down onto the track. Only the fast, streamlined karts have aerofoils.

Chassis
The basic frame on which the body of a vehicle is built.

Direct drive kart
A kart without gearbox.

Dummy grid
A marked area off the track where the karts line up in their correct position before starting their warm-up lap.

Enduros
Kart races on the road racing courses in the United States.

Formula E
The international class for 250 cc karts with gearboxes.

Formula K
The international class for 135 cc direct drive karts.

Grid
Area behind the starting line where the karts line up in rows before the start.

Hairpin bend
A bend, shaped like a hairpin, where the track turns back in the opposite direction.

Long-circuit racing
Karting on motor racing circuits.

Pit
The area where mechanics can work on the karts.

Pre-finale
The qualifying laps run to determine final grid positions.

Short-circuit racing
In Europe, karting on specially built tracks of 750 to 1,500 m (820 to 1,640 yd) a lap.

Slicks
Smooth racing tires.

Speedway
In the United States, karting on dirt oval tracks of $\frac{1}{10}$ to $\frac{1}{5}$ (160 to 322 m).

Sprints
In the United States, karting on twisting, short asphalt tracks.

Streamlining
Smooth aerodynamic bodywork that reduces air resistance.

Index